IMAGES OF AVIATION

AVRO ANSON

Waiting for war. Patrolling over the Scottish coastline in May 1939 is K6298 of No.233 Squadron based at Leuchars near St Andrews, Scotland.

IMAGES OF AVIATION

AVRO ANSON

HARRY HOLMES

First published 2000 by Tempus

Reprinted 2017 by
The History Press
The Mill, Brimscombe Port,
Stroud, Gloucestershire, GL5 2QG
www.thehistorypress.co.uk

British Library Cataloguing in Publication Data.
A catalogue record for this book is available from the British Library.

ISBN 978 0 7524 1738 7

Typesetting and origination by Tempus

Printed in Great Britain by TJ International Ltd, Padstow, Cornwall

Contents

Acknowledgements

The Avro Anson does not feature in the ranks of the famous or more glamorous types of aircraft, but for many it does hold a special place in our hearts and I am most grateful to the many aviation historians who, over almost fifty years, have provided many of the photographs appearing in this book. Because the aircraft was used in such great numbers over a long period the book could have been filled many times over, but I hope that the selection of pictures will be enjoyed and, no doubt, bring back memories of those rather quieter days of aviation. My grateful thanks go to my old friend George Jenks, who I met at Avro over forty years ago and who is always willing to help with any project. Others who deserve my thanks include Chris Ashworth, Hugh Cowin, David Earl, Brian Forward, Don Hannah, Eric Harlin, Mike Hooks, Maurice Marsh, Peter Marson, Jim Oughton, Brian Robinson, Ray Sturtivant, Eric Taylor, Andy Thomas, John Wegg, N.D. Welch and Ray Williams. Not to be forgotten are friends who have passed on including Peter Keating, Hubert Parrish, Arthur Pearcy and John Rawlings. Always an excellent source of aircraft photographs are Brian Pickering of Military Aircraft Photographs and Brian Stainer's Aviation Photo News. Air Britain's Anson File by Ray Sturtivant was also useful for cross-checking Avro company records.

Harry Holmes
Middleton
Manchester
January 2000

Introduction

After visiting the United States early in 1933, G. Woods Humphrey, managing director of Imperial Airways, met Sir John Siddeley who was chief executive of the Armstrong Siddeley Development Company Limited to discuss his ideas for a fast, long-range, mail-carrying charter aircraft. Woods Humphrey had been impressed by the Boeing 247 twin-engine monoplane airliner he had seen on a visit to the Boeing Company, but that aircraft was too large for the Imperial Airways requirement. On 18 May 1933, A.V. Roe & Company Limited in Manchester received the full specification from Sir John who gave Avro chief designer Roy Chadwick the task of designing an aeroplane to meet the airline's requirements.

By 1 August 1933, Chadwick's enthusiasm for the project had produced a complete design study for a four-passenger aircraft, powered by two Armstrong Siddeley Cheetah radial engines, giving a cruising speed of 165mph with a range of 700 miles. The study was fully approved by executives of Imperial Airways and work commenced on the design of the Avro 652.

Chadwick, along with Roy (later Sir Roy) Dobson, had visited the Fokker factory in 1928 to study the company's method of producing a basic fuselage structure of welded steel tubes which held wooden formers covered in fabric. A number of Avro aeroplanes followed using this system, including the Avro 618, a licence-built version of the Fokker F.VII high-winged trimotor airliner. Using this production method Chadwick designed the new aircraft with a one-piece wooden mainplane in the low wing configuration with two 270hp Cheetah V engines providing the power. The stated requirement for a retractable undercarriage was met by a gearing system which, after 140 turns of a handle in the cockpit, moved the wheels forwards and upwards into the engine nacelle.

Half of the wheel itself was exposed and this feature became a great plus point in later years if this type had to make a wheels-up landing, as very little damage would be caused to the airframe because the aircraft was able to run freely on its still retracted undercarriage. The pilot's cockpit was fitted with dual control and each of the four passengers would have a circular window.

The contract for two Avro 652s was signed by Imperial Airways at the Avro Headquarters in Newton Heath, Manchester, on 16 April 1934. It was while the Type 652 was in the design stage that the Air Ministry invited companies to submit studies for an aircraft to fill the new role of general reconnaissance, and after seeing the specification Chadwick was delighted to find that it was close to that of his airliner design. He and his team were soon at work preparing a military version to be known as the Type 652A.

The first Avro 652 for Imperial Airways took to the air on 7 January 1935 in the capable hands of Avro's deputy chief test pilot F.B. 'Tommy' Tomkins followed by the usual first flight report that the aircraft had 'excellent "Avro" handling qualities'. Tomkins was given the honour of making the maiden flight as his boss, chief test pilot 'Sam' Brown, was overseas demonstrating the Avro 626 in Brazil and Chile, both exercises being highly successful.

The first aircraft was named 'Avalon' and the second 'Avatar', although the latter was quickly changed to 'Ava' before delivery when it was found that the name was something quite unmentionable in a certain European language! The delivery to Imperial Airways at Croydon on 11 March 1935 did not pass without problems as both aircraft left the Avro airfield at Woodford immediately climbing into thick cloud which continued for their flight down to Surrey. In the first 652 was test pilot S.A. 'Bill' Thorn with Bill Andrews, one of Chadwick's design staff, while Tomkins piloted the second machine accompanied by assistant works manager Jimmy Kay, but the poor weather separated the aircraft and the planned arrival of them both together was put in jeopardy. The airline's welcoming party decided to wait for the arrival of their new aeroplanes, but experienced more excitement than they had bargained for as 'Avalon' made a perfect landing with the wheels still retracted! It was a crew error as Thorn and Andrews had completely forgotten the retractable undercarriage. Apart from the bent tips of the metal propellers very little damage was done, and the aircraft was unceremoniously pushed by willing helpers into the Imperial Airways hangar, rolling nicely on its still retracted wheels.

Both the Avro 652s gave excellent service to Imperial Airways, particularly on the Croydon to Brindisi, Italy, route which was flown over 100 times without mishap. The aeroplanes were sold to Air Service Training Limited in July 1938 to be used as navigation trainers, but after the outbreak of the Second World War they were pressed into military service, eventually joining the Royal Navy at Lee-on-Solent in July 1941. After a short period of flying the first aircraft was grounded to become an instructional airframe while the second machine was damaged beyond repair in October 1941 after being struck by a landing Chesapeake aircraft at its Hampshire base. A smaller version of the Avro 652 was to have Genet Major engines and a fixed spatted undercarriage, but although a mock-up was completed and some component production undertaken the aircraft, known as the Type 660, did not proceed.

Chadwick's changes in the design of the Avro 652 for the general reconnaissance aircraft required by the Air Ministry were almost in place when Avro received a communication to request that the tender for the new aircraft should be marked 'urgent'. The process was speeded up with the tender being submitted to the Air Ministry on 19 May 1934. Avro was informed that the design and tender had been accepted in a letter dated 21 September 1934 with one prototype aircraft being ordered.

The new Avro 652A would be powered by two Cheetah VI engines each giving 295hp with an estimated range of 600 miles at 160mph. The main armament could consist of a mid-upper manually-operated gun turret or a single Lewis gun on a swivel mounting fitted in the cabin roof directly above the main spar. The pilot would have a single forward-firing Vickers machine gun fixed on the port side of the aircraft. A bomb load of 360lb could be carried.

The prototype Avro 652A took off from Woodford for its maiden flight on 24 March 1935 piloted by Bill Thorn, and after a number of flights at both Woodford and Martlesham Heath the aircraft was flown to the Coast Defence Development Unit at Gosport, Hampshire, for a series of trials in competition with the DH89M, a military version of the Dragon Rapide. The trials, which took place between 11 and 17 March 1935, proved that the Avro machine was superior in range and endurance and it was selected for the RAF's requirement. The prototype appeared in the New Types Park at the Hendon RAF Display on 29 June 1935 before being flown back to Woodford by Sam Brown.

The Air Staff Requirement No.23 was issued on 27 August 1935 for full development of the Avro 652A with the name Anson in honour of Lord George Anson, British Admiral of the Fleet in the eighteenth century, but this selection caused a rift between the Air Ministry and the Admiralty as the latter believed that it was their right to use names of famous seafarers. An agreement was reached so that it would not happen in the future.

It is widely reported that the first order for the Anson received on 1 July 1935 was for 174 aircraft, but the Avro company records state that Works Order 4825 was for 162 machines. However, trials on the prototype at Martlesham Heath, Suffolk, had not been trouble-free, as much criticism was made of its rudder control and stability. Chadwick had already been working to counteract the problems after earlier reports and an extended tailplane, larger fin and the deletion of the horn balance on the rudder solved the problems. The Cheetah VI engines would be replaced by the more efficient Cheetah IXs when they became available early in 1936, but this installation would require the engines to be mounted three inches further forward. Constant centre of gravity changes were also overcome giving an all-round improvement to the aircraft's handling.

With the adoption of the Anson, which conformed with Air Ministry Specification 18/35, an alternative design, the Avro 664, did not proceed. The production prototype of the Anson made its first flight on 31 December 1935, piloted by Geoffrey Tyson, and differed from the first aircraft by the introduction of a continuous line of cabin windows in place of the square windows of the original machine.

A milestone in the history of the RAF was reached on 6 March 1936 when the first monoplane entered squadron service with another 'first' being the use of a retractable undercarriage as Ansons joined No.48 Squadron at Manston, Kent. At that time the Royal Australian Air Force (RAAF) was showing great interest in the aircraft with Avro receiving an initial order for thirty-eight of the type, which was soon followed by a contract for a further ten Ansons. In order to maintain the interest by the RAAF twelve aircraft were taken from the RAF contract and delivered to Melbourne, Australia, on the SS *Orani* on 19 November 1936. The first machine was test flown by Wing Commander A.W. Murphy at Laverton on 2 December 1936 before entering service with No.2 Squadron, RAAF, just seven days later.

During 1936 two further contracts were signed by the Air Ministry, the first for seventy-eight, and the second for thirty-five machines. While the second batch was under construction changes were made in the pilot's windscreen with a steeper design and opening direct-vision panels. Schrenk-type flaps were introduced to improve the gliding angle and metal-framed ailerons were added. Anson Mk I deliveries to the RAF were steadily increasing and by the time of the 1937 Display at Hendon five squadrons including Nos 206, 220, 224, 233 and 269 took part in a mass formation fly-past.

Interest from other overseas countries was beginning to materialise with the Avro sales office at the Newton Heath factory having to increase its staff to meet the demand. Three aircraft were taken from the third RAF batch for the Finnish Air Force with an extra one being diverted to the Estonian Air Force. The Egyptian Army Air Force ordered one Anson for a proposed bomber/transport role with a higher take-off weight and other modifications. This aircraft was delivered in civilian markings in November 1936 with the designation Avro 652 Mk II with its entry door on the port side as in the original design, as opposed to the starboard location on the Anson. However, the aeroplane was clearly an Anson Mk I. Orders were received from Ireland and Turkey with the latter's contract for twenty-five being reduced when the war started after only six had been delivered. Twelve of the order were actually flown out in British civilian markings to help the Greek Air Force in June 1939, but some of these were destroyed or captured by the Germans. Five were able to escape to Egypt where they joined the RAF. Six Ansons were transferred to the Royal Iraqi Air Force by the RAF in 1939, serving until 2 May 1941 when the Rashid Ali uprising saw them destroyed.

As the war clouds gathered in 1939 orders were placed for 1,332 aeroplanes, and increased by a further 1,000 after war had been declared. More aircraft were transferred to the RAAF and others to the South African Air Force.

Although obsolescent at the start of the Second World War, the Anson still provided RAF Coastal Command with a potent offensive aircraft and this was proved as early in the war as 5 September 1939 when one of No.500 Squadron's 'Faithful Annies' bombed a German U-boat. Aircraft from this squadron carried additional machine guns in the side windows and the commanding officer of No.206 Squadron, Squadron Leader W.E. LeMay, experimented with a

20mm Hispano cannon fitted below the cabin floor of his personal Anson. The Germans were also well aware of the aircraft's capabilities as, in an early report, it was stated; 'The value of aircraft keeping our boats submerged and denying them surface mobility cannot be forgotten. Ocean convoys are given close air support by Ansons to the convoy dispersal point at 15° west (about 200 miles west of Ireland) with coastal and Scandinavia convoys also being so covered.' In September 1939 a No.269 Squadron Anson operating from Montrose, Scotland, shot down a Dornier Do.18 flying boat, and after being attacked by three Messerschmitt Bf.109s, three Ansons on patrol over the English Channel were able to destroy two 109's and damage one as the fighters continually overshot the throttled-back Avro's. On 11 July 1940 a Heinkel He.59 seaplane was forced down into the Channel by a No.217 Squadron aircraft flying from St Eval, Cornwall. The German crew of four were rescued from their dinghy and taken prisoner. Other enemy aircraft falling victim to the guns of Ansons were a Heinkel He.115 seaplane, a Heinkel He.111 bomber and a Messerschmitt Bf.110 twin-engine fighter.

As the Lockheed Hudsons began to arrive from the United States to equip the Coastal Command units the Anson was withdrawn from front line service, but was already in line for another important task, this time as an aircrew trainer. The British Commonwealth Air Training Plan had been launched on 18 December 1939 and the Anson had been selected as one of the main types required by the scheme. Large production orders followed as the aircraft would be serving in Canada, South Africa, Southern Rhodesia, New Zealand and Australia. The Avro company had already moved its headquarters from the Newton Heath plant to the massive new factory at Chadderton near Oldham, but as the production requirements of the Manchester bomber and later the Lancaster would take up all of the available floor space, it was decided to move the whole of the Anson production to the new shadow factory at Yeadon (now Leeds-Bradford airport). The first Anson produced by the Yorkshire facility rolled off the line in June 1941 and by July 1942 this type was being flown away from Yeadon at the rate of twenty-six per week. A steady increase in production late in 1943 and the first three months of 1944 reached a peak of 135 aircraft per month. By the end of the war a total of 3,881 Ansons had been produced, but from VJ Day until production was ended in December 1945 a further seventy-six aircraft were completed making Yeadon's overall Anson production 3,957.

A large number of the older Anson Mk Is were shipped to Canada for the Training Plan, but a shortfall in the eventual requirement, due to aircraft being allocated elsewhere and the acute shortage of Cheetah IX engines, forced urgent action resulting in a production scheme being established in Canada. Because of the lack of engines new versions evolved including the Mark II, which was locally built and equipped with Jacobs engines giving 330hp. This type later included a moulded plywood nose and a Dowry hydraulic undercarriage and flaps and was adopted by the US Army Air Corps as the AT-20. The Mark III was a British-built airframe fitted with the Jacobs engine, while the Mark IV was a British airframe with Wright Whirlwind engines. Ansons V and VI were other Canadian versions while Marks VII, VIII and IX were reserved for new versions from that country, but not used. The last two completed versions had Pratt & Whitney engines with fuselages constructed of moulded plywood.

Back in Britain the Anson X made its appearance with no turret and a strengthened floor, designed for communications and ambulance work. It was to be in two versions with the Series 1 having Cheetah IXs, but the old-style hand-crank undercarriage and the Series 2 having Cheetah XIX engines and a hydraulic undercarriage. The Mk X was mostly associated with the Air Transport Auxiliary (ATA) which had the role of ferrying new aircraft from the manufacturers to their respective services during the Second World War. Their Ansons flew nearly ten million miles with only eight fatalities in the whole of that period, prompting one ATA official to remark; 'The Anson's characteristics were so free of vice and its engines so reliable that it produced an accident rate which, it is believed, has not been bettered in full commercial work.' In September 1944 ATA Ansons delivered a continuous airlift of supplies to the British Second Army fighting in Belgium and it is reported that some of the aircraft were so fully packed that the pilot had to get into his seat through the port side sliding cockpit window!

As earlier types soldiered on in various types of training for all classes of aircrew, the new aircraft were being designed specifically for communications and freight carrying. Marks XI and XII had a deeper fuselage, hydraulic undercarriage and flaps with the only difference being in the powerplants. The Mark XI had the Cheetah XIX while the Mark XII had the Series XV engines.

At the end of 1943 the Brabazon Committee met to make various recommendations for the types of aircraft needed for civil transport after the war. One of these was a twin-engined feeder aircraft with dimensions close to those of the Anson, and Chadwick's team was soon at work designing an aircraft to be known as the Avro XIX. This type, described as a feeder liner/communications aircraft, had a completely redesigned interior and cabin windows, being built in two main versions with either wooden or metal wings and tailplane. After Avro modified an Anson XII into a nine-seat feeder aircraft this machine was operated by the Associated Airways Joint Evaluation Committee, and deemed suitable for civil airline operations. The RAF ordered twenty-five of the new version, converted from Mk XIIs, and a contract was then placed for a further 160 to be known in service as the Anson C.19.

Throughout the aircraft's later life there was always confusion in the use of the Mark number in either Roman or Arabic numerals with some company documents mixing the two. One example quoting a Mk XII early in the brochure then two pages later describes the Mk 12! Mark numbers to the XIX (C.19) included Mks 13 and 14 reserved for Turret Gunnery aircraft; Mks 15 and 16 for Navigation and Bombing Training aircraft with Mk 17 not being allocated. None of these five versions were built. The designation Anson Mk 18 was given to a batch of twelve Bombing, Gunnery and Radio Trainers for the Royal Afghan Air Force while the Mk 18C was used as a Civil Aircrew Trainer for the Indian Government.

In 1946 the Rhodesian Air Training Group was formed and with it the need for a navigation trainer. Avro modified the basic C.19 design to be equipped with the latest navigational instruments plus a glazed nose as additional training for bomb aiming and underwing racks for small practise bombs, this version being designated the T.20. The Anson T.21 built to Air Ministry Specification T.25/46 was basically a home-based T.20, but without the glass nose and bomb racks. A small number of T.20s remained in the United Kingdom in reserve status. The last Mark of the Anson was the T.22 which was designed as a radio trainer, and fifty-four were supplied to the RAF.

After the war, apart from those Ansons specifically designed for civil operations, many ex-military aeroplanes gave excellent service in the steadily growing airline industry. Others were converted to survey or photographic aircraft both at home and overseas.

After seventeen years of continuous production, the last Anson, a T. Mk 21, was test flown by Avro's chief test pilot Jimmy Orrell on 13 May 1952 before being handed over to the RAF by the Company's managing director Sir Roy Dobson two weeks later. Ansons continued to serve in the RAF until their official retirement on 28 June 1968 when the six aircraft of the Southern Communications Squadron marked the occasion with a formation flypast over their home base at Bovingdon, Hertfordshire.

As the last aircraft was being handed over it was quoted as the 11,020th of the type to be produced, but this figure was found to be erroneous as one batch had been duplicated and the actual figure was 10,996.

With only a handful remaining, mostly in static condition, the sight and sound of an Anson in the air cannot fail to give onlookers a twinge of nostalgia. The Air Atlantique and Woodford's own restored aircraft are soon to be on the UK's Air Show circuit. With examples still flying over sixty-five years after the type first took to the air, Roy Chadwick could not fail to be proud of the much-loved 'Faithful Annie'.

First of many! Taken in October 1934 at Avro's Newton Heath factory, Manchester, the first Avro 652 takes shape. It could not have been envisaged that this design would be the basis of almost 11,000 Ansons which would follow and as G-ACRM the aircraft would make its first flight from Woodford on 7 January 1935.

One

The Avro 652 and 652A Anson

The second Avro 652 G-ACRN was named 'Avatar' for delivery to Imperial Airways, but the name was quickly shortened to 'Ava' when it was found that the former meant something quite unmentionable in a certain European language!

A good illustration of the port-side entry door and the large windows, one for each of the four passengers.

During a test flight of G-ACRN piloted by 'Tommy' Tomkins, famous aviation photographer Charles Sims took some excellent shots from an Avro 626 being flown by Avro's chief test pilot 'Sam' Brown.

'Avalon' was soon repaired after a wheels-up landing at Croydon and test flown by Thorn before being officially handed over to Imperial Airways. The horn-balanced on the rudder was later deleted.

The highly polished engine cowlings are evident in this shot as the Imperial Airways mechanics prepare the aircraft for a service flight to Brindisi, Italy.

A close-up of the opening nose of the Avro 652 which allowed mail sacks to be stowed in the forward part of the aircraft. The nose cone also incorporated a landing light.

The only Avro 652 Mk II was built for the Egyptian Government and first flown by 'Sam' Brown on 13 October 1936, then delivered in the civilian markings SU-AAO the following month. The aircraft was basically an Anson I, but with the entry door on the port side as in the original Type 652 design. Initially used by the Egyptian Army Air Force, it was later transferred to the Royal Egyptian Air Force and given the serial number W204.

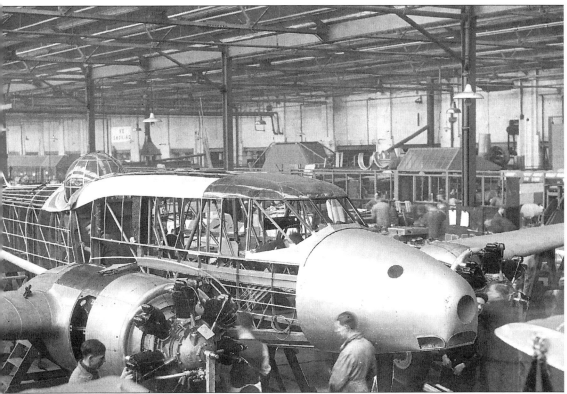

The prototype Avro 652A under construction at Newton Heath in January 1935. The aircraft was completed then dismantled and transported to Woodford for reassembly and flight testing.

As all of the prototype's early photographs were lost in the large fire at Avro's Chadderton factory in October 1959, it was fortunate that the late Sandy Jack was on hand to catch K4771 on its final engine run before the maiden flight on 24 March 1935. Note the Avro Tutor and one of the original hangars, which still forms part of the Woodford Flight Sheds.

The prototype in pristine condition after its arrival at Martlesham Heath for service evaluation

The production prototype of the Avro 652A, now named Anson, made its first flight on 31 December 1935 with Geoffrey Tyson in command. A feature of many pre-war Ansons was the use of the serial number on the upper surfaces of the wing.

A side-view of K6152 taken as a series of photographs shot from various angles of all new aircraft types. The large all-round windows, which differed from the first aircraft, are evident.

Another view of the production prototype on rock hard ground and the remains of a January 1936 snow shower.

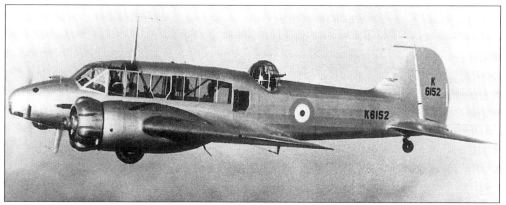

Seen on an early test flight, K6152 provided much evaluation data before the aircraft was passed to the service. It was written-off after a crash-landing at Catterick, Yorkshire, on 13 October 1939 while serving with No.220 Squadron.

The fourth production Anson at Newton Heath before its journey to Woodford for assembly and delivery to No.48 Squadron at Manston, Kent, in March 1936.

The wings for K6155 joined the convoy of components for transporting to Woodford's assembly hangar. This aircraft served until October 1940 when a forced landing prompted its withdrawal from training duties to become the ground instructional airframe 2368M.

It was a proud day for the Royal Air Force and No.48 Squadron at Manston, Kent, when the unit received its Avro Anson Is. This type was operated by the Squadron until October 1941 when the changeover to the Lockheed Hudson was complete.

The Central Flying School (CFS) at Upavon, Wiltshire received K6163 in April 1936 and the new aircraft is seen here in formation with other types of that recently formed unit including an Oxford, Hart, Tutor and Fury.

A fine in-flight study of K6159 before it joined No.48 Squadron at Manston as the unit speedily built up its Anson fleet which eventually totalled eighty. The Squadron was, at that time, a training unit which introduced aircrew, particularly navigators, to the role of general reconnaissance over water.

Down in the drink! An early casualty in the aircraft's career was K6166 which crash-landed in the sea six miles off the Kent coast on 25 June 1936. The aircraft stayed afloat and was towed into Tankerton harbour near Whitstable where crowds of onlookers gathered to see it. After various tests the machine was reduced to spares.

An early overseas customer for the Anson was the Finnish Air Force with the first of three ordered, AN-101, leaving Woodford on its delivery flight on 27 September 1936. This aircraft served for the next eleven years. The Anson became instantly famous in Finland when, during an Air Show at Malmi Airport, Helsinki, the aircraft was put through a full aerobatic routine which included two loops!

Three Ansons of No.215 Squadron stationed at Driffield, Yorkshire, head back to their airfield after a familiarisation flight in February 1937.

The Irish Army Air Corps ordered two Anson Is with A19, the first aircraft, seen here at a very wet Woodford just before its delivery to Baldonnel aerodrome on 20 March 1937.

Since the design had been announced the Royal Australian Air Force (RAAF) had shown great interest in the Anson, resulting in an initial order for thirty-eight aircraft. To maintain interest the RAAF were allocated twelve aircraft from an RAF batch with the first aircraft A4-1 (ex-K6212) being test flown in Australia on 2 December 1936.

The steady arrival of the Avro Anson in squadron service prompted a series of formation photographs of the receiving units. Here, No.217 Squadron gather over the Channel in a flight from their base at Boscombe Down.

Flying from No.220 Squadron's station at Bircham Newton, Norfolk, is a selection of Ansons, including K6209 which has still to have a gun turret fitted. This aircraft was transferred to the South African Air Force (SAAF) in November 1940 and served until 17 March 1942 when it was badly damaged in a night crash-landing.

Scotland was the home of No.269 Squadron for most of the time the unit was equipped with Ansons and this nice line-up was photographed at Abbotsinch in 1937.

Aircraft of No.217 Squadron prepare to take off for an exercise over the Channel.

Thick mist covered the Cleveland hills on Saturday 11 September 1937 when K8778 of No.233 Squadron crashed into Hunters Hill near Guisborough, North Yorkshire. The aircraft was on a cross-country exercise from its base at Thornaby when the crash occurred, fatally injuring Pilot Officer L.W. Lowden and his three crew members.

A busy scene at Avro's aerodrome, Woodford, in December 1937. The aircraft being refuelled include the Irish Army Air Corps Anson A21, the Yugoslavian C.30 autogiro No.1 and an Avro 626 destined for Portugal.

A private snapshot of the prototype Anson K4771, at Hendon in October 1938. In the background are the Auxiliary Air Force hangars belonging to No.601 (County of London) Squadron and No.604 (County of Middlesex) Squadron.

Boscombe Down was the home of No.51 Squadron when this photograph of K6281 was taken in 1938. The unit soon received Whitleys with the Ansons being transferred to other squadrons and this particular machine shipped to Canada in July 1941.

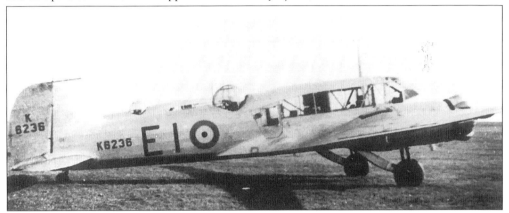

The School of Air Navigation's K6236 at Manston in 1938. The aeroplane's eventual wartime service was short, as she ended her days on the beach at South Shore, Blackpool on 30 September 1940 after a forced landing while serving with No.1 School of General Reconnaissance at Squires Gate.

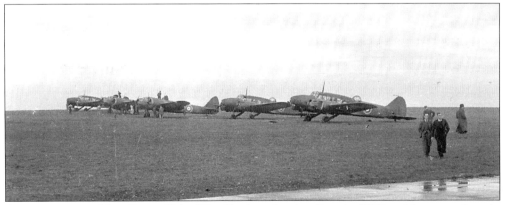

Ansons were steadily rolling off the Woodford production lines in 1939 and here are three in company with two Avro-built Blenheim Is awaiting test flights. Wartime production of Ansons was transferred to Yeadon until the end of hostilities when it returned to the Manchester area.

His Majesty King George VI visited Newton Heath to see the Anson production lines in March 1939. To the King's left is Sir Frank Spriggs, chairman of the Hawker Siddeley Group, while to his right and partly hidden is Roy (later Sir Roy) Dobson, managing director of Avro.

The 'HU' coding was used by No.220 Squadron at Thornaby until the outbreak of war when they switched to 'NR' with the arrival of their Lockheed Hudsons. The aircraft here, K6200, was lost en route to Canada in the Norwegian freighter SS *Horda* when it was torpedoed and sunk by U-97 under the command of Leutnant Udo Heilmann on 24 March 1941.

Two

The Mark I in war
and beyond

The 'office' of an Anson I showing the excellent all-round vision and the pilot's gun sight for his fixed forward-firing machine-gun.

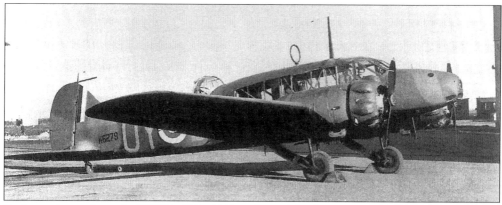

Early wartime colours for K6279 of No.48 Squadron. After being employed on anti-submarine patrol the unit's Ansons were replaced by Lockheed Hudsons, with K6279 being transferred to the South African Air Force (SAAF) on 18 June 1941 to become No.3122. It was badly damaged in a crash-landing near East London on 9 November 1942 and was Struck Off Charge (SOC) six months later.

Another aircraft from an RAF contract to be sold abroad was K8741 which became No.158 of the Estonian Air Defence Force. It was completed by Avro at Woodford on 15 October 1936 and reportedly destroyed in the German invasion of Estonia in 1941.

A long way from its home base at Wick, Scotland, is No.269 Squadron's K8760, photographed during a visit to Cranwell early in 1940. The red and blue fuselage roundel had been carried since April 1939, but returned to the standard marking in 1940.

Seen at No.45 Air School, Oudtsoorn, Northern Cape, South Africa, is No.1134 of the SAAF. As K8768 the aircraft had served with a number of RAF units before being transferred on 14 September 1940. The machine gave excellent service to both countries for over ten years before it was eventually sold for scrap in October 1947.

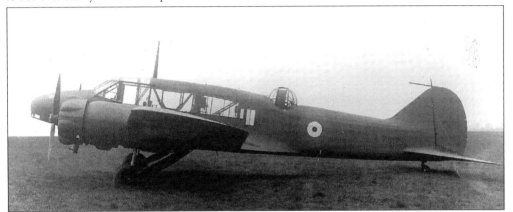

Another long serving Anson, L7906 is pictured here at Woodford, just off the production line. It served with various training units until it was SOC on 4 May 1945.

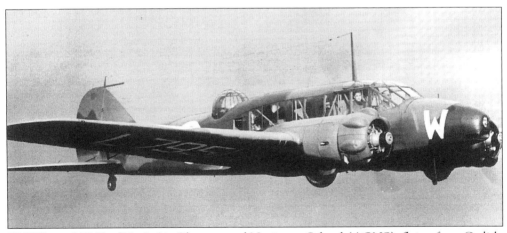

W-William, L7951 of No.3 Air Observer and Navigator School (AONS), flying from Carlisle early in 1940. Transferred to the SAAF as No.1135 on 8 September 1940, it was last reported at No.7 Air Depot, Queenstown in 1946.

The London School of Flying at Elstree owned the Anson I G-AMDA before it was sold to Peter Thomas of the Skyfame Museum on 30 August 1963. It was repainted with its original wartime colours with the serial number N4877, but with the spurious code-letters 'VX-F' to represent an aircraft of No.206 Squadron. Its war service was confined to training units and it was never in an operational squadron.

A later shot of N4877 as 'VX-F'. The aircraft was rebuilt to static condition after a bad landing at Staverton on 2 November 1972 and is now preserved at the Imperial War Museum, Duxford.

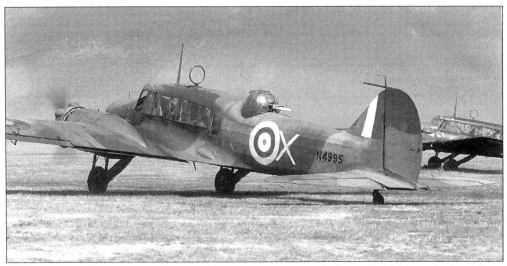

Operated jointly by Nos7 and 76 Squadrons at Upper Heyford was N4995 with both of these units merging to form No.16 Operational Training Unit (OTU) on 8 April 1940. This aircraft was also involved in a fatal crash. Flying with No.1 (Observer) Advanced Flying Unit (OAFU) at Wigton, it flew into Cairn Hill, Ayrshire, on 3 February 1943.

Probably the most well-known Anson in SAAF service was No.3158 as it was the only one of its type ever fitted with floats. The non-flying machine seen at Congella Dockyard, Durban, was used to instruct prospective Sunderland flying boat crews on aircraft-handling on water. Wearing the code-letters 'RB-Z' of No.35 Squadron, SAAF, the Anson had served in the RAF as N4927 before its transfer to South Africa on 14 January 1941 and conversion to a seaplane in 1943.

After pre-war service with No.148 Squadron, N5085 served with a number of RAF units until the war's end. Photographed at Upwood in 1941 the aircraft carries the code-letters of No.17 Operational Training Unit.

Another Anson to find its way to South Africa was N5106 seen in the markings of No.48 Squadron, RAF, operating from Hooton Park, Cheshire in early 1941. The aircraft was officially handed over to the SAAF, becoming No.3137, but was damaged beyond repair in a crash-landing on 25 June 1942 after both engines failed during a landing approach.

Missing on convoy escort was N5227 of No.500 Squadron which was lost on 30 May 1940. It was photographed at Detling earlier in1939.

The description 'Mad Poles' usually described the Polish airmen's aggression towards the Germans, but N5331 of No.6 Air Observer and Navigator School (AONS), flown by one of their number, cannot be more than ten feet off the ground! Despite flying like this, the aeroplane did survive the war.

A rare photograph of the 20mm Hispano cannon installation below the cabin floor of an Anson of No.206 Squadron. Squadron Leader W.E. LeMay reportedly used the weapon to great effect against German E-boats in the Channel during 1940.

A line-up at No.10 Service Flying Training School (SFTS) at Tern Hill, Shropshire, in 1940. The whole unit went to Canada to become No.32 SFTS at Moose Jaw in November of that year. Aircraft No.52 in the photograph, N9650, went to Canada on 11 June 194,1 retaining its British serial number throughout the war.

This No.269 Squadron Anson N9673 ended its days at Wick, Scotland, when it crashed on take-off for an anti-submarine patrol on 21 March 1940

Photographed at Ringway, Manchester, while awaiting the maiden flight of the Avro Tudor I on 14 June 1945, N9828 taxies past the new airliner. This Anson remained on the RAF inventory until February 1955 when it was sold for spares.

Avro deputy chief test pilot 'Bill' Thorn, who flew the prototype Avro 652A on its maiden flight, is pictured here during an inter-factory flight in an Anson. He was promoted when 'Sam' Brown retired in 1945, but lost his life in the crash of the Tudor II at Woodford on 23 August 1947. Famous chief designer Roy Chadwick also died in the accident.

The large number of Ansons being shipped to the Commonwealth Air Training Plan caused a shortage of Cheetah IX engines, with Canada fitting either Jacobs or Wright Whirlwind motors to fill the requirement. The British-built Anson Is equipped with the 300hp version of the latter engine became known as the Mark IV, with the trials conducted in England on R9816, seen here in October 1941 at the Aircraft and Armament Experimental Establishment (A&AEE), Boscombe Down, Wiltshire.

Another view of R9816 showing the smooth engine cowlings and Hamilton-Standard propellers.

A close-up of the new powerplant of the Mark IV at Woodford. The aircraft did go to the Royal Canadian Air Force (RCAF) as No.10257 on 19 March 1942. It flew a number of trials with various units including an evaluation by the USAAF at Wright Field and was eventually disposed of in February 1945.

Having made its first flight as R9883 in the cold of Woodford this aircraft was soon on its way to join the Royal Australian Air Force (RAAF) at No.2 Aircraft Park on 28 October 1940. Seen here at Mascot Airport, Sydney, eighteen years later as VH-AGA of Adastra Aerial Surveys after a long career with the RAAF, it was sold in January 1947 to become VH-AVT. It was re-registered as 'AGA' in April 1957 and eventually taken off the register on 18 July 1962. It was donated to the Camden Museum of Aviation and is preserved in wartime colours as the fictitious 'N9151'.

Presentation aeroplanes were normally combat types, so it was unusual that an Anson should be chosen to represent an organisation named the 'Silver Thimble'. Serving with the SAAF it was appropriate that the aircraft was named 'South Africa'.

An excellent flying shot of two aircraft of No.48 Squadron in 1941 with T-Tommy, W1887, which served with six training units after leaving No.48 and survived the war to become the instructional airframe 6556M on 12 May 1948. A-Apple, N9908, was similar, but was SOC on 28 September 1944.

Having arrived in Australia, like many others W2083 was without its gun turret, but this photograph was taken early in 1942 showing the new addition. It spent most of its service with the RAAF's General Reconnaissance School (GRS) at Laverton and Bairnsdale before it was sold for scrap in November 1947.

Looking sad and out to grass at Bankstown, Australia, in 1963 the Anson I W2599 is destined for preservation. The aeroplane arrived in Australia and went straight to No.2 Aircraft Park at Bankstown on 10 October 1941. Sold to Adastral Aerial Surveys on 30 July 1948 the aircraft never received a civilian registration and remained unused. It is strangely devoid of markings apart from its ex-RAF serial number and the nose number '73', a leftover from its days with No.6 Service Flying Training School (SFTS) at Mallala, South Australia.

Blue Line Airways at Tollerton, Nottingham, rescued G-AJBA from the liquidation of its previous company and restored it to the UK civil register on 21 July 1949. As AX409 the aircraft served with three different RAF training units before going into the civil market. Sadly it was destroyed by fire at Montgenèvre, France, on 10 February 1950 while being operated by Eagle Aviation Limited.

One of the first Ansons to be allocated to the RNZAF was NZ409 which had been DG694 when it came off the Yeadon production line. The benefit of the protruding wheels is shown again as the aircraft is towed away for repair after a wheels-up landing.

Looking like a model in this view, NZ412 was part of the second batch of Ansons for the RNZAF. Arriving on the SS *Mahia* on 5 August 1942, this aircraft was also Yeadon built as DG701 before going to the SGR at Omaka. After its war service NZ412 was put into storage, but was restored in 1948 serving with the Air Navigation School at Wigram until 1954 when it was sold for scrap.

The Middle East Communication Squadron (MECS) was stationed at Heliopolis, Egypt, where this photograph of DG963 was taken in 1944. The aircraft was destroyed in a crash on take-off at Benina, Libya, on 20 September 1945.

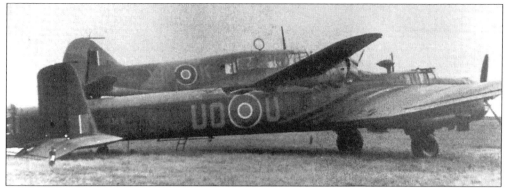

A poor but interesting shot of DJ104 which bounced on top of the Whitley N1369 at Kinloss, Scotland, on 20 October 1943 after a heavy landing. Although both belonged to No.19 Operational Training Unit they carry code-letters of different Flights. The Anson belongs to 'F' Flight.

This Anson, VH-AKI, photographed in 1947, went to Australia to join the RAAF on 27 July 1942 as DJ165. After serving with a number of training units, it was sold on the civilian market on 20 August 1946, and registered seven months later. However, after two months on 6 May 1947, it was registered to British & Continental Limited, a UK air charter operator, as G-AJSD. The aircraft had already been scrapped at Southend when its registration was closed on 13 July 1950.

A recovery team from No.83 Maintenance Unit at Woolsington, Newcastle, survey the wreck of DJ453 on Cross Fell in the Western Pennines after its crash on 18 February 1943. The aircraft, belonging to No.4 Air Observer School, had taken off from West Freugh, Scotland, for a cross-country navigation exercise when the pilot, concerned about heavy icing, descended to ease the problem. The aircraft was off course and hit the rising ground, with only minor injuries to the four crew members.

Leaving Avro's Newton Heath factory on an RAF low-loader is DJ456 which was destined for South Africa. Joining the SAAF as No.4253, the aircraft served with No.61 Air School at George, Cape Province, before going into storage and facing eventual disposal in January 1946.

Based at Thornhill, Southern Rhodesia, in 1948, DJ563 coded 'Z-C' was operated by No.3 Air Navigation School of the RAF. The aeroplane saw wartime service with No.10 (Observer) Advanced Flying Unit at Dumfries, Scotland, before it was shipped to Southern Rhodesia.

Undergoing maintenance at Burnaston is G-AIPA, operated by Derby Aviation Limited on behalf of the Canadian Aero Service in 1959. As EF866 the machine had flown with No.5 AOS, and Nos 62 and 80 OTUs before going onto the civil register on 22 October 1946 and being eventually scrapped at Burnaston in 1961.

Jurby, Isle of Man, was the home of EG276 while it served with No.5 Air Observers School, RAF. Transferred to the Royal Norwegian Air Force (RNAF) on 17 January 1947 and allocated the serial W-AF, the aircraft served until 1950 before it was sold to Yugoslavia as YU-ABU in March 1951. Nothing is known of it after that date.

Miles away from home is VR-SDK of Nanyang Airways Limited at Kallang, Singapore. As EG436 it served with No.3 School of General Reconnaissance at Squires Gate, Blackpool, then joined the Empire Radio School (ERS) at Debden, Essex as 'TDE-A' for post-war service. It received British civil registration G-ALXF in January 1950, but went to Singapore in March 1952. Note the change in windows, including the incorporation of those from a de Havilland Rapide.

One of the Ansons used by the Fleet Air Arm in the early 1950s was EG496, seen here while being operated by the Station Flight at RNAS Bramcote, Warwickshire, which became HMS *Gamecock* after the war, home base of No.1833 Squadron, RNVR. During the war the aeroplane was flown on air-sea rescue duties by No.278 Squadron. Its service with the Royal Navy ended when it was SOC on 24 January 1954.

Seen here at Laverton, Victoria, near the end of the war, EG504 had arrived in Australia on 12 July 1943. The aircraft carries the code-letters of No.67 Squadron, RAAF, but also the wrong 'EC' prefix to its serial number. Presumably this mistake was made when the aircraft was repainted after a taxiing collision with a refuelling truck on 23 May 1944. The machine was scrapped in May 1948.

Before going to Kenya in January 1950 to become VP-KHP, this aircraft also had a modification with individual passenger windows in place of the normal 'glasshouse' type. First registered in the UK as G-AHMZ on 9 May 1946, the aeroplane's RAF service career from 1943 to 1945 was spent at the Staff Pilot Training Unit (SPTU) at Cark, Cumberland with the serial number EG637.

It was a long way from Yeadon, Yorkshire, to Digri, India, where EG645 was photographed in 1945. Belonging to No.1331 Conversion Unit (CU) and stationed at Risalpur, the aircraft was mainly involved in ferrying duties. After the unit was disbanded early in 1946 EG645 was SOC in India on 23 April 1946. In this shot the aeroplane is in the colours of the South East Asia Command (SEAC) which features the dark and light blue national markings.

With its national markings and serial number EG689 crudely painted over, G-ALFD awaits new colours after its purchase from the Ministry of Supply by Rollasons of Croydon in October 1948. While being operated by Transair Limited, one of its later owners, the aircraft was written off in a non-fatal accident when it hit buildings while landing in fog at Melsbroek, Brussels on 17 February 1952.

Photographed in the January 1943 snow at A&AEE, Boscombe Down, LT112 was the prototype for the fitting of the Bristol B.1 gun turret for the combined role of navigation and gunnery trainer. The all-up weight of the Anson had increased steadily since its early days and the fitting of this heavy turret led to overheating of the engines resulting in modifications including larger, smoother engine cowlings. This machine went to the French Air Force on 27 July 1946, but its fate is not known.

Retained by Avro for development work, LT764 had its Bristol turret removed to become the prototype of the Anson X which was classed as an 'Interim Communication and Ambulance Aircraft' The 'interim' title was given to the aircraft as it still had the standard fuselage, but was temporarily fitted with equipment for the forthcoming Mark XI. The aircraft was later flown by the Air Transport Development Flight, but was SOC on 7 March 1949.

Seen here well tied down is MG227 which was transferred to the Royal Netherlands Air Force on 19 February 1947 to become No.D-25 based at Twenthe until it was disposed of on 15 August 1952. Its RAF service was with the Staff Pilot Training Unit at Cark, Cumberland.

Notable for its all-yellow colour scheme and Bristol turret, No.D-19 was another of the twenty-five Ansons which joined the Royal Netherlands Air Force during 1946-1947. As MG283 the aircraft had served in the RAF with No.8 Air Gunnery School (AGS) at Evanton in Scotland, where it arrived in the middle of 1943 as one of the replacements for the unit's dreaded Blackburn Bothas.

Looking pristine after a new paint job in 1951, MG467 had been used mainly as a trials aeroplane, including laminar flow research tests. Its last assignment was with the Bombing Trials Unit at West Freugh, Scotland before it was sold to an unknown buyer on 11 March 1955.

A nostalgic scene at Ringway, Manchester on 21 September 1951, showing the Fingland Airways Anson I G-AKFM parked near the pre-war petrol pumps at No.3 Hangar. The machine was sold to Hunting Aerosurveys Limited and was eventually transferred to their East African division in Nairobi, Kenya, with the registration VP-KME. The aircraft was retired in 1956 and was ex-RAF MG495. Mark XIX type windows have been fitted to the aeroplane

A nice landing shot of the Air Transport Auxiliary MG582 complete with 'invasion stripes' required for trips to the Continent in the latter half of 1944. The aircraft was written off when bad weather forced it down into a field next to Boot Railway Station in Cumberland on 11 October 1945.

After RAF service as MG588 this aircraft was purchased by the College of Aeronautics, Cranfield, on 11 November 1946. As the College used a number of aircraft for airborne experimental work, G-AIPC returned to Avro almost immediately after the sale to be converted to a trials aeroplane, including a variable incidence tailplane and attachments for the fitting of a variety of tail fin sections. It was retired from flying on 26 August 1955.

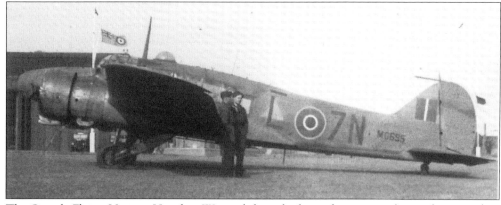

The Signals Flying Unit at Honiley, Warwickshire, had a wide variety of aircraft engaged in signals development flying. This aircraft had flown its early days at No.2 Gunnery School, Dalcross, Scotland, but MG695 spent most of its life in signals and radio work before being sold for scrap in March 1949. The photograph was taken at Honiley in May 1946.

With its civilian registration G-ALEM hastily applied over its service serial number, MG756 was another of the Ansons purchased by Rollasons in 1948. However, the aircraft was never flown again and the registration was closed on 26 July 1949 after the machine was broken up.

Looking patched up and rather sad, the ex-Fleet Air Arm Anson MG860 is seen here at Burnaston in 1956 after being bought by Derby Aviation from Air Service Training at Hamble. The intention was to put the aircraft onto the civil register, but it was reduced to spares that same year.

After RAF operations as MG901, this aircraft was sold into the civil market as G-ALUM, registered to Transair of Croydon on 29 July 1949. It was sold in Denmark and became OY-DYC on 8 April 1954, as seen here, still with Transair titles. On 16 February 1956 it crashed due to engine failure in poor weather near Grená on the Kattegat coast, and was destroyed.

A rare flying shot of an RAAF Survey Flight Anson MG982 operating from Lowood, Queensland in 1944. The aeroplane arrived in Australia in May of that year and operated until 13 October 1947 when it was sold to a civilian organisation to become VH-BME on 14 January 1949. The aircraft appears to have flown little in its civilian guise, and was eventually grounded on 13 January 1950.

One of the most interesting Ansons in Australia was VH-BAF of Brain & Brown Airfreighters, seen here in 1972. It started life as MH120 for the RAAF on 20 March 1944 and was released to the civil market in August 1953, but not registered until five years later. It was on aero mapping duties when it crashed on 7 October 1960, but was completely rebuilt using tapered metal wings from the Anson XIX VH-BIX and Cheetah XV engines. It was restored to the register with B & B at Moorabbin on 16 August 1963, flying until 2 October 1974 when it was withdrawn from service. Sold to a private owner in January 1984 it was made airworthy once more. When it first appeared on the civil scene the registration VH-BLP was reserved for it, but was not taken up.

In the 1950s Burnaston aerodrome near Derby was an interesting place for the aviation enthusiast, as Derby Aviation overhauled and converted a variety of aircraft. The Anson OY-ADB, which was being converted for a Danish operator, was a source of interest from August 1956 when it arrived, until it gradually deteriorated to scrap as the order was not taken up. The aircraft had spent its service life as MH153 with the Fleet Air Arm. In the background are two Mosquitoes being converted for Spartan Air Services of Canada.

After an interesting wartime career in the 2nd Tactical Air Force and the ATA, MH182 was sold as G-ALXC on 16 January 1950. Operated by the Federated Fruit Company of Speke, Liverpool, the aircraft became well-known around northern Britain, but in June 1954 it was sold to an Irish air charter company as EI-AGQ.

This is the same aircraft as it appeared in 1956 before it was repossessed by the Federated Fruit Company and restored to the UK register. It was flown again until the Certificate of Airworthiness (CofA) lapsed in March 1961, but the aeroplane received dispensation for a ferry flight to Southend one month later. It was reported to have been sold, but was never flown again and was scrapped at Southend in 1968.

Enthusiast Maurice Marsh took this interesting photograph of NK328 at Walsall aerodrome on 13 April 1947. The aircraft had been operated by the Blind Landing Experimental Unit (BLEU), but the radar aerials appear to be of the Air to Surface Vessel (ASV) type. This Anson was sold for scrap on 16 January 1951.

After RAF service with Nos8 and 11 Air Gunnery Schools the nearest aircraft, NK482, joined the French Air Force on 21 September 1945. Photographed at Pau in 1948, the second Anson in the line-up, No.27, is LT833.

Destined for the RAF as NK484, this aircraft was flown to the Avro facility at Langar to be prepared for service with the Portuguese Air Force, with delivery by the company being made on 1 April 1946. Initially used by the transport unit at Portela, the eleven Ansons delivered gave excellent service and it was reported that two were still operating in 1960.

The RAF College at Cranwell operated NK563 as 'FAG-A', seen here in August 1948. The aircraft went to Thorney Island, Hampshire, in 1949 to take part in the Michael Dennison film 'Landfall', a story about a wartime Coastal Command pilot. After completion of the film, the aircraft was sold for scrap on 28 March 1950.

Loaves of bread, barrels of beer and newspapers were flown daily to the troops on the Continent in 1944 and here NK670 of No.83 Group Support Unit has just made a delivery during August of that year. After the war it served as a navigation trainer, declared surplus in March 1949.

An excellent view of NK941, one of the Ansons used by AST on the Royal Navy contract. It had served with a number of units in the Fleet Air Arm before being taken over for the Hamble-based radar training organisation. When the Air Service Training Ltd (AST) contract ended in November 1953 the machine was transferred to No.750 Squadron at St Merryn in Cornwall until it was SOC on 2 April 1955.

The Iraqi Air Force acquired thirty-three Anson Is after the end of the war and this rare photograph shows No.181 of No.7 Squadron based at Baghdad in 1950. Little is known of their use and eventual fates.

Three

The conversions and Marks XI and XII

Avro used G-AGNI as a demonstration aeroplane, but it was sold in July 1947 to Southampton Air Services and moved on again just three months later when it joined Universal Flying Services Ltd, as that company bought out the former's assets. The aircraft was lost when it crash-landed in the sea off Bradda Head, Isle of Man on 11 June 1948.

MG159, seen here at Yeadon in 1944, had a varied career ahead of it. It was taken from the Anson I production line to become the development aircraft for the Mark XI, but was soon updated to the Mk XII. The aeroplane was registered G-AGNI (see previous page) and later converted to an Avro Nineteen (sometimes referred to as the Anson XIX).

The prototype Anson XI, NK870, was evaluated by the A&AEE at Boscombe Down before going to the RAF Balkan Air Force on 19 January 1945 to be at the disposal of Marshal Tito of Yugoslavia.

Another aircraft with an interesting career was G-AGLB, first flown as NL152 on 5 September 1944 before being converted to VIP standard for the RAF Air Attaché in Madrid. The machine went on the civil register on 28 November 1944, but after service in Spain returned to Avro for conversion to Mk XIX, completed by October 1945. It served the Air Attaché in Belgrade until its registration was closed on 17 November 1948 when it returned to general RAF service as NL152. After various postings its last role was with the Station Flight at Abingdon, Berkshire, before it was retired in October 1963.

A company photograph showing the location of the baggage compartment on the starboard side. Although allocated its civil registration in November 1944, the war was still very much in progress hence the red-white-blue stripe under the registration letters to denote the aeroplane's civilian status. The stripes were also applied to the wing letters, but used only red and blue.

The Anson XII NL175 was one of the batch of 800 laid down at Yeadon to become Mark Is, but conversions were introduced during the build process producing a mixture of Mks X,XI and XII. This aeroplane, photographed by the Ministry of Aircraft Production in December 1944, was allocated to No.85 Group Communications Squadron, serving in Belgium and Germany before being SOC in July 1947.

Operating as a flying radar laboratory the Mk XI G-ALIH was owned by Ekco Electronics Limited and flown from Southend, Essex, from 1954 to 1968 after conversion from a passenger aircraft. Its service life as NL229 included a period based in Copenhagen, flying with the RAF Mission to Denmark. After retirement from Ekco its future looked secure as it was presented to the Newark Air Museum at Winthorpe airfield, Nottinghamshire in November 1970, but sadly, just six months later it was destroyed by fire after vandals broke into the museum compound.

Seen here among the wreckage of broken-up Ansons, the future looks bleak for the Mk XII PH535 at Silloth, Cumberland, in 1960. Obviously, LOT 1 had not been purchased and the aeroplane was destined to go the way of hundreds of other types in No.22 Maintenance Unit's 'graveyard'. The machine had served with a number of RAF units including a period with the Berlin Communication Flight before its rather inglorious end.

Avro converted the unused NL246, Mark XI, into a VIP aircraft for use by an Air Attaché. Registered as G-AGLM to the Secretary of State for Air, the aircraft retained its original camouflage colour scheme of November 1944. It was transferred to the Ministry of Civil Aviation at Croydon in July 1945, but joined the RAF in the following February as NL246.

Completed as a VIP aircraft, the Anson XII PH616 was seen at Yeadon before it departed on its long journey to Panama to become the personal aircraft of the British Air Attaché. The aeroplane never left Central America as it was sold in Mexico, as XA-GOX owned by Aerovias Reforma, in June 1947.

An air-to-air shot of PH616 on a pre-delivery test flight, taken by Avro staff photographer Paul Cullerne. Nothing is known of the aircraft after its sale to Mexico.

An interesting modification to PH624, an Anson XII, was the fitting of continuous Mark I type windows. The aircraft belonged to the Central Navigation and Control School when it was photographed at Shawbury, Shropshire, in 1958. The machine then served with No.61 Group Communications Flight (GCF) before it was released and sold as scrap on 29 February 1960.

The Mark XII PH769 saw service with ten RAF units before spending its final days in Wiltshire with RAF Colerne's Communications Flight, being Struck Off Charge on 30 July 1956.

Refuelling at RAF Church Fenton, Yorkshire, in 1956, is the Mark XII PH782. The aircraft belonged to the Armament Practice Station at Acklington, Northumberland, but was reduced to spares after a take-off accident at its home station on 14 November 1956.

A landing shot of PH814, originally a Mark XII before it was withdrawn and returned to Avro at Bracebridge Heath, Lincolnshire for conversion to Mk XIX, RAF designation C.19, on 26 February 1951. It returned to service on 21 May 1952 and it is seen here going into its home base at Hendon, London, as 'CB-F' of the Metropolitan Communications Squadron. The aircraft's last home was Leconfield, Yorkshire, where it belonged to the Station Flight. It was SOC on 7 May 1964.

PH816 was a well-travelled aircraft, another Mark XII converted to a VIP Avro Nineteen on 15 November 1945. Its first stop was Lisbon for the use of the Air Attaché with the civilian registration G-AGPU, but it was returned to the Ministry of Supply and resumed its RAF serial number PH816 on 4 February 1948. The machine was fitted with a modified glazed nose and operated by various trials establishments before joining the Royal Aircraft Establishment at Farnborough, Hampshire, where it was photographed in 1955. It was scrapped at the end of October 1957.

One of the hangars used for Anson overhauls at the Avro Maintenance and Repair site at Bracebridge Heath, with two aircraft shown. The one on the right is the Mark I NK841 which had been completely overhauled after arriving from the 2nd Tactical Air Force on 20 August 1946, while the left machine, the Mark XII PH546, had commenced its overhaul on 7 December 1946.

The fuselages of Anson XIIs showing the extent of the overhaul process at Bracebridge Heath. The airfield there closed after the First World War so aircraft requiring overhaul were flown into RAF Waddington and towed the 500 yards to the Avro facility.

The Ansons overhauled at Bracebridge had the full treatment, and this photograph shows the Engine Shop in June 1947 with fitters working on Cheetah XVs.

Four

The Canadians

An excellent flying shot of the CF-EZW named 'Comox Queen' of Queen Charlotte Airlines Limited of Vancouver, British Columbia, which operated with the airline from January 1947 until it was retired in October 1950. In the RCAF as 12547 the aeroplane had served with No.7 AOS and No.1 School of Flying Control, both of which were stationed at Portage la Prairie, Manitoba.

Outside the De Havilland Aircraft of Canada factory at Downsview is N9913, the first Anson Mk I to be assembled in Canada from sections manufactured at Newton Heath. The aircraft became 6001 of the RCAF, going into service in February 1940, later being converted to a Mk III by the fitting of Jacobs engines to replace the original Cheetahs. After serving as number 3542, the machine was SOC on 9 February 1945.

No.6049 was another early arrival in Canada being assembled from R3527 and photographed here at No.4 Air Observer School at London, Ontario. The machine later became a Mk III through the shortage of replacement Cheetah engines.

Seen at No.5 Service Flying Training School (SFTS) at Saskatoon, Saskatchewan, before its change to Mk III, is 6140, ex-W1517. The aeroplane survived the war to be disposed of in March 1946.

An RAF trainee climbs aboard for yet another exercise and, no doubt, it would not be too long before he returned to the UK to join an operational squadron. The marking on the upper wing panels was yellow. This colour also extended from the turret on the upper fuselage to the base of the fin and the tailplane.

Moncton, New Brunswick, was the home of No.8 FSTS when 6358 was photographed there in 1942. Despite the hard training and poor flying conditions on occasions, the Ansons in Canada had an excellent safety record and this machine, ex-W1915, also survived the war.

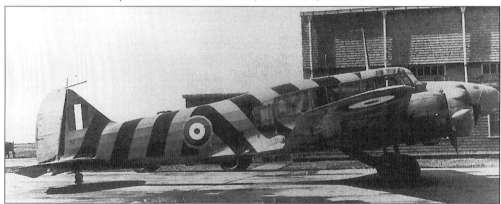

This yellow and black striped Anson at No.8 SFTS, Moncton, still carried its British serial number W2531 underwing, although it had been allocated RCAF 6759. This Canadian official photograph was taken on 16 September 1941.

Recognised by the smooth cowling of the Jacobs engine, the Mk II 8515 of No.18 FSTS is seen in the snow at its base at Gimli, Manitoba. The all-yellow training colour scheme also assisted search aircraft if any machine was forced down in the snow.

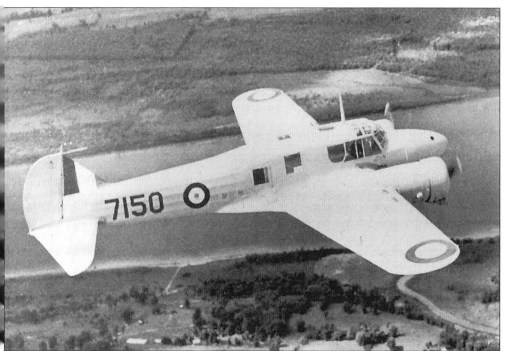

Flying over the Souris River is 7150, an Anson II of No.17 SFTS at Souris, Manitoba in 1944. The aircraft had spent some time with the RCAF Test and Development Unit before its allocation to the training school.

The first Canadian designed Anson V seen soon after roll-out. Built with a moulded veneer fuselage and powered by Pratt & Whitney engines, the aircraft was designed as a navigation trainer. This particular aeroplane, No.11581, flew with a number of units until it was retired in June 1947.

Having served with the Eastern Air Command and No.1 General Reconnaissance School, both based at Summerside on Prince Edward Island, the Mk V 11806 is reported to have been lost at sea on 11 September 1944. As another aircraft from the same unit suffered the same fate on that day, it is possible that the aircraft collided.

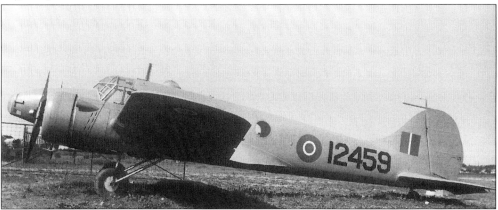

Awaiting disposal in June 1946, 12459 went onto the Canadian civil register as CF-EHK, but was little used and the registration was closed in November 1950.

The Mk V 12511 from No.18 SFTS at Gimli, Manitoba, in 1944. Besides its training duties the aircraft was relocated to the Station Flight and only served at Gimli until it was SOC on 5 September 1946. Although it was put up for sale it had no takers in the civilian market.

The only Anson Mk VI, 13881, served as the prototype for this Mark which was to be a gunnery trainer. The aeroplane had the moulded veneer fuselage and Pratt & Whitney engines as in the Mk V, but was fitted with a Bristol gun turret. After being evaluated by the RCAF's Test and Development Establishment no further trials were undertaken as the war was drawing to a close and the type was not required for service. The aeroplane was SOC at Trenton, Ontario, in January 1947 and is reported to have been purchased for the civil market as CF-WAC although this does not seem to have been taken up.

The Anson's toughness was demonstrated on 7 December 1943 when JS167 was on approach to Gimli, Manitoba, when JS193, also in the traffic circuit, collided with and locked onto the lower aircraft. By some excellent airmanship by the captain of JS167 both machines landed safely. The two aircraft were repaired and completed their service with No.18 SFTS until retirement came in August 1946.

A busy scene with a mixture of Ansons and Harvards at No.8 SFTS at Moncton, New Brunswick, in July 1943. The aircraft in the foreground, the Anson Mk II JS190, went on to serve with No.18 SFTS before it was SOC on 19 August 1946.

Fifty Anson Mk IIs were supplied from Canada to the USAAF for navigator and bombardier training with the American designation AT-20. The Federal Aircraft-built machines were flown to Wright Field in Ohio with the official hand-over date being 16 September 1942. The pictured aircraft had the serial number 43-8223 with the code R422, as seen late in 1944.

The Federal AT-20 43-8215 coded K-174 was photographed at Kearney Army Airfield, Nebraska, in 1943, but little is known of the use of Ansons by the Americans. Presumably they would have been operated as a stop-gap until the Beech AT-11 Kansan took over the advanced training role.

Looking smart in a dark blue and white colour scheme CF-EKM was owned by the strangely-named Pringle's Baby Chick Express until it was cancelled from the register in June 1950. The Anson V completed its RCAF service as 12032 with No.5 AOS at Winnipeg, Manitoba, in April 1945 and was put into storage before being sold to the civil owner just over a year later.

Lome Airways of Toronto flew the Anson Mk V CF-FXH until 9 September 1951 after buying it from the Aero Tool Company in June 1948. The machine had been 11630 with the RCAF.

One of the of Spartan Air Services Anson fleet was CF-HXA which was acquired by them in November 1954 directly from RCAF storage. It appears that the aircraft went straight from the manufacturers into store and did not serve with an operational unit. The small bomb-like device under the fuselage is a magnetometer for the geographical survey work carried out by Spartan.

After service with No.2 Air Navigation School (ANS) at Charlottetown, Saskatchewan as 11904, the aircraft was stored until it was made available for the civil market in June 1954. It was eventually bought by Austin Airways of Toronto in April 1957 and flown by that company until the CofA expired on 27 June 1974. The aeroplane was presented to an aircraft museum at Gimli for restoration and display. In this photograph the aircraft also carries a magnetometer 'bomb' for surveying.

A number of Canadian Ansons are displayed in various museums throughout Canada and this Mk II is on show at the excellent facility of the Nanton Aircraft Museum at Nanton, Alberta, where it was photographed by the author's wife, Betty.

Five

The Avro Nineteens

Avro XIXs at Baldonnel on delivery to the Irish Army Air Corps on 4 April 1946. With serial numbers 141 to 143 they were 'maids of all work' as they were used for training, passenger, freight, communications and reconnaissance duties. No.143 was damaged in a landing accident on 8 May 1953 and reduced to spares, No.142 had a similar accident and became a ground instructional airframe. No.141 was withdrawn from service to replace No.142 when it was scrapped. In the background is the Anson Mk I No.44 ex-N4866, delivered to the IAAC on 2 February 1939.

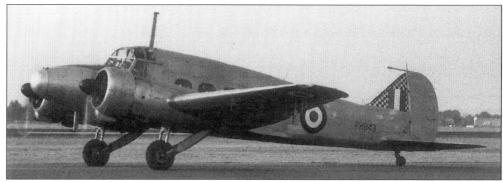

Looking very smart with its chequered fin is PH843 the Anson C.19 which ended its days in January 1969 after being released by the Western Communications Squadron at Andover, Hampshire. The Avro Nineteen was born out of the feeder-liner specification from the Brabazon Committee of 1943 when requirements for post-war airliner types were being formulated. When the RAF ordered the aircraft after the war the type became known as the Anson C.19 in service.

Another of the early C.19s was PH858 which was operated for a year as G-AIIA by the British Air Attaché in Belgrade. Shown here in RAF Transport Command colours, the aircraft had a white top, blue cheatline and dayglow orange fuselage bands. It served until it was SOC in November 1967.

Photographed in 1963 while operated by the Station Flight at RAF Gaydon, Warwickshire, TX155 was presented to the Liverpool Children's Hospital at Heswall when its flying days were over in July 1971.

Fresh from the Yeadon production line in February 1946 is PH861. The aeroplane's career was short, for as it was returning to the UK from service with the East Africa Communications Flight at Eastleigh, Kenya in October 1947, it developed a serious mechanical problem and was scrapped at Ciampino airport, Rome.

After spending a long period serving in Germany, TX157 returned to the UK for duties with a number of RAF units. It was sold to the Avro-Whitworth Division of Hawker Siddeley Aviation Limited at Baginton, Coventry, with the registration G-AVCK, but after languishing for two years it was scrapped in November 1969.

On approach to Runway 2-4 at Ringway, Manchester, on 4 July 1967 is TX183 arriving from the Handling Squadron at Boscombe Down. After retiring this aircraft was earmarked for preservation, going to the Shuttleworth Trust at Old Warden, Bedfordshire, before moving to the Imperial War Museum at Duxford. It is now thought to be in Scotland undergoing restoration.

Operated by Headquarters No.1 Group, TX186 arrives at RAF Waddington for the Battle of Britain Day on 19 September 1964. The aircraft survived for a further four years before being sold for scrap after serving with the Northern Communications Squadron (NCS) at Topcliffe, Yorkshire.

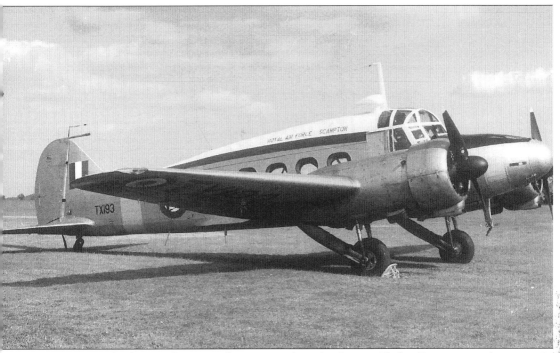

RAF Scampton was the home of TX193 when it served on the Station Flight. During its early service the aircraft was fitted in the VIP configuration before use by the Air Attaché in Prague, but reverted to the standard interior for going to the Reserve Command Communications Flight at White Waltham, Berkshire, in August 1949. After use by a number of units the machine ended its service with the NCS at Topcliffe in July 1967.

Photographed from an RAF Devon, the Anson C.19 TX214 of the Metropolitan Communications Squadron(MCS) is seen making the last flight from Hendon when the airfield was closed in November 1957 due to the encroachment of a housing development scheme. At the time of the picture, the MCS was moving to RAF Northolt. The aircraft was preserved and is now on display at the Cosford Aerospace Museum. Note the removal of the emergency exit window to allow photography.

The remains of VL300 lie in the scrap dump at RAE Llanbedr, Wales, when it was written off in a heavy landing there on 7 October 1960. The stripped-off titles were probably collected

as souvenirs before the aeroplane disappeared completely. Almost everything usable has been stripped off for spares.

Ansons were regular visitors to the Avro airfield at Woodford, bringing crews for the collection of Vulcans and Shackletons during the 1950s and 1960s. Aircraft also returned to Avro for modification or repairs and here a delivery crew are about to board TX230 for the return flight to their home base. In the background is the Shackleton MR.3 XF711 coded 'L' of No.201 Squadron, which arrived for modernisation on 11 January 1962.

Parked on Woodford's sloping ramp is VL351 during a visit in June 1964. The airfield was the destination of many Ansons, not only on crew movement duties, but also on cross-country training flights when aeroplanes would just happen to arrive about lunch time! Even in later years it was not unusual to see a Canberra, Phantom, Jaguar, Harrier or Tornado stopping by for lunch.

Obviously someone had not read the instructions for marking application as VM307 carried an entirely non-standard serial number and fin flash paint scheme. The aircraft, which belonged to RAF Wyton's Station Flight, was under the control of Bomber Command and the paint sprayer seems to have followed the manual for bomber-style markings of the period, 1953.

The RAF College at Cranwell, Lincolnshire, operated VM315 for a short period before it moved on to the Central Flying School (CFS). Aircraft flown by the College could be recognised by the pale blue rear fuselage band, as seen in the photograph. After service with the CFS it was released for preservation in May 1963, but its current status is unknown.

Photographed in 1949 the C.19 VM392 'QU-L' of the Northern Ireland Communications Flight at Aldergrove used wartime-style codes along with Proctors and Oxfords of that unit.

Awaiting the axeman at RAF Shawbury, the once proud VM334 is parked with others with no reprieve in sight. In the background can be seen the fin of an ex-No.24 Squadron Hastings, put out to grass with the arrival of the unit's Hercules. VM334's last owners were No.11 Group Communications Flight at Leconfield, Yorkshire and the aircraft was eventually sold for scrapping on 5 August 1970.

An RAF Anson C.19 outside the Control Tower and No.1 Hangar complex at Ringway, Manchester, in 1946. The offices on the extreme left of the picture were used by No.14 Ferry Pool of the ATA until it was disbanded shortly after the war's end. These buildings disappeared with the arrival of the modern terminal which was opened in December 1962, and the airport has continued to grow ever since.

Although never serving with the R.Neth.AF, No.D-26 was bought for £200 from RAE Llanbedr to represent the Ansons which served in Holland. Ex-VM352, the C.19, was delivered to Soesterberg Air Base on 28 May 1971 for display by the Air Force Museum.

In 1956 the Irish Air Corps (IAC) separated from the Army to become an independent organisation and it was after the changeover that a policy was devised for historic aircraft preservation. The Avro XIX No.141 was released from its instructional duties to be preserved for display. It was moved from Baldonnel in July 1993 to the Irish Aviation Museum in Dublin.

Originally registered in Britain as G-AGUI, No.121 was one of two delivered to the Imperial Ethiopian Air Force for use by the Emperor. It arrived at Liddetta airfield, Addis Ababa on 28 January 1946, but after service there it returned to the UK register for Sangster and Short at Croydon in January 1948. It never flew again and was reduced to spares with the remains of the airframe burnt on site in February 1953.

Under the designation Anson Mk 18C, VT-CXT is seen here soon after completion at Woodford on 11 March 1949. Basically a Mk 19, the aircraft was the first of twelve ordered by the Indian Government as civil aircrew trainers.

The yellow and black Indian Mk 18C is photographed on its first test flight on 8 April 1949. VT-CXZ is in the very capable hands of Avro chief test pilot Jimmy Orrell.

Photographed in Malta on 14 May 1948 while on delivery to the Afghan Air Force at Kabul is this Anson Mk 18. The aircraft was one of twelve ordered from Avro six months earlier and, like the Mk 18Cs for the Indian Government, this model was very similar to the Mark 19.

The busy production line in Woodford's New Assembly hangar in July 1948 shows three of the Afghan Air Force Ansons in their final stages with RAF Anson T.21s following them down the line. In the far bays can be seen a number of Avro Tudor airliners.

A July 1945 photograph of Avro's own communications Anson, lovingly known in the company as 'Aggie-Paggie' because of its registration letters. Originally a Mk XII, the aircraft had gone onto the UK register just one month earlier, but was not classified as an Avro Nineteen until January 1947. The colour scheme was royal blue and silver.

An interesting shot of a famous Avro trio taken on 20 October 1960, showing G-AGPG, now in a silver colour scheme, the prototype Avro 748 and a Vulcan B.2 on the Flight Sheds ramp at Woodford.

The interior of G-AGPG showing the six-seat configuration with a toilet situated at the rear of the cabin. The wing main spar running across the cabin floor is in the foreground with the hat rack and emergency exit also evident.

After being transferred from Avro to Skyways Coach Air in July 1961, G-AGPG was sold by them to Ekco Electronics in 1967. It was eventually presented to the Historic Aircraft Aviation Museum at Southend in April 1972, but the demise of that organisation saw it auctioned to a French owner although it was then abandoned. The sad remains were purchased by the British Aerospace (ex-Avro) factory at Chadderton for restoration to static display for the North-West Museum of Science & Industry in Manchester, but work has yet to commence. This photograph from the late 1960s shows the large radar nose fitted by Ekco.

One of the early Avro Nineteens on the register, in May 1946, was G-AGZT used by the Ministry of Civil Aviation. It was sold to Channel Air Services of Jersey in January 1953 and was owned by them when photographed by Ken Rutterford at Croydon on 27 July of that year. After transfer to Fairways (Jersey) Limited, the aircraft made a wheels-up landing at Croydon on 3 January 1957, but was never repaired.

G-AHIG was a Railway Air Services aircraft, taken over by the British European Airways (BEA) and photographed in the colours of its new owner in 1947. After a number of operators the machine ditched in the sea off Calshot, Hampshire, on 6 August 1955 when owned by Fairways.

Railway Air Services operated the largest fleet of Avro Nineteens, with fourteen aircraft flying out of Croydon but, on 1 February 1947, BEA took over the former and its fleet of aircraft. This aircraft, G-AHIB, was sold three months later and, after a number of owners, ended its days on the scrap dump at Wymeswold, Leicestershire, in 1961.

The Avro Nineteen metal-wing Series 2 prototype G-AHKX was originally sold to Smiths Instruments Ltd, and registered on 18 May 1946. It was still owned by them when photographed at Staverton, Gloucestershire, in June 1958.

After serving with Meridian Airmaps of Shoreham, Sussex, from March 1961 until May 1965, G-AHKX moved on again, this time to Treffield Aviation Ltd, of Sywell, Northamptonshire, where it was pictured in 1966.

Kemps Aerial Surveys bought G-AHKX in January 1967. It flew for them for six years before joining the Strathallan Aircraft Collection in May 1973. The aeroplane came up for auction on 14 July 1981 and was purchased by the author on behalf of the Manchester Division of British Aerospace. This photograph shows the aircraft on the day of the auction.

After a long and thorough restoration, originally by apprentices and in later years by retired members, G-AHKX is, at the time of writing, about to take to the air once more. The picture shows the aeroplane outside the 1916 hangars of A.V. Roe & Company Ltd, which were moved to Woodford in 1924 when the aerodrome at Alexandra Park, Manchester, was closed.

Ansons undertook a new task in 1947 when G-AKDU was fitted with special spray equipment to become part of the pest control unit in Southern Rhodesia. In this photograph the spray tubes can be discerned between the undercarriage legs. Although it had civil markings the aircraft was flown by RAF crews, and after a landing accident at Heany aerodrome on 30 July 1950, the machine was reduced to spares.

The Avro Nineteen G-AKFE was ex-RAF VP512 which was used by the Air Attaché in Vienna and later had a similar role in Belgrade. The civil registration was closed in April 1956, when the aircraft was returned to RAF service with its original serial number to serve with the 2nd Tactical Air Force. It was SOC on 5 August 1959.

After serving as the C.19 VM360 with a number of trials units including the A&AEE at Boscombe Down, this aircraft was sold as G-APHV in November 1957. Equipped as a survey machine, the photograph shows the aircraft when owned by BKS Air Survey Ltd, in 1963. After service with other operators the aeroplane went to the Strathallan Aircraft Collection in 1973 and was eventually passed on to Museum of Flight at East Fortune, Scotland in August 1977.

Carrying the Red Cross insignia while operating for Mercy Missions during the Biafran food relief crisis G-AWMH had been retired as TX227 from the RAF in August 1968. It flew numerous food aid missions before it crashed near the River Cess, Liberia, fortunately without fatalities, on 20 June 1969.

PH845 wears transitional colours after being released by the RAF to become registered as G-AVTA in August 1967. It was owned by Tippers Air Transport at Halfpenny Green, Staffordshire, but for some reason remained unconverted and was scrapped in 1968.

An interesting colour scheme for G-AWML includes identification stripes reminiscent of wartime invasion markings, but although the aircraft was destined for the Biafra 'Save the Children' role, it never left the UK. The ex-TX166 was sold to the Historic Aircraft Museum at Southend, Essex, in July 1968 and that organisation's insignia can be seen on the aeroplane's fin flash. It was scrapped at Weston-Super-Mare, Somerset in mid-1970.

One of four Ansons which flew on the German civil register was D-IDAM which had an interesting career after first appearing as G-AHIK in April 1946. It served with BEA and Starways at Liverpool until sold in Sweden as SE-BUI in June 1952, eventually going to Germany in June 1956. It was retired in 1962 with the main sections being seen at Frankfurt in mid-1968.

When photographed at Southampton Airport in 1960, the background of EC-ALF was obscure. After finding the Avro build number, 1277, research showed that it was one of the first to be delivered to Railway Air Services in November 1945 with the registration G-AGUX. While serving with a later owner the machine crashed in the Spanish Sahara in December 1951 and was written off. It was recovered by a Spanish company, rebuilt and flown again from Madrid in June 1955 as EC-ALF. It continued to operate until 1963 when it was retired from flying.

This Avro Nineteen, registered in Iran and photographed at Teheran in 1960, started life as VM305, an Anson C.19 for the RAF. While in production it was converted to the prototype T.20 navigational trainer and evaluated at A&AEE Boscombe Down. It was sold in April 1959 to Air Couriers of Croydon before going to W.S. Shackleton Ltd in March 1960. The dealer then sold it to Iran, but, on 24 September 1960, EP-CAA was damaged beyond repair in a non-fatal accident.

In mid-1946 Belgian Congo Railways ordered two Avro Nineteens from the manufacturers. This group of pilots who arrived for crew training and delivery includes three who served with the RAF during wartime. On the extreme right is ex-Squadron Leader Remi van Lierde, a fighter ace who destroyed forty V-1 flying bombs while flying a Hawker Tempest, with No.609 Squadron.

An Avro photograph of the two aircraft on their delivery flight to Brussels, before heading for the Congo. The first aircraft OO-CFA was later registered to SABENA as OO-DFA in June 1950, then after private ownership as OO-VIT, it was sold to Kemps Aerial Surveys in April 1971 as G-AYWA. The second machine OO-CFB was destroyed in a crash at Kindu, Belgian Congo, on 7 April 1948.

Misrair of Cairo operated SU-ADN, which went onto the Egyptian register in June 1946, named 'Tanta'. Converted by Avro at Yeadon from the C.19 PH860, it was originally G-AGWD for the Ministry of Civil Aviation at Gatwick, but was transferred to the Egyptian Government with the one-off RAF serial VN889 in February 1946. It was last heard of operating in 1949.

Well-known to the author as G-AHXK 'Mancunia' of Sivewright Airways of Manchester in the 1948 to 1952 period, this aircraft was sold to Hawker Aircraft Limited to operate from their airfields at Langley, Buckinghamshire, and Dunsfold, Surrey, in August 1952. Ten years later the aeroplane went to Australia for Nicholas Air Charter as VH-RCC, operating until 27 February 1964 when the registration was cancelled after an accident.

Six

The Trainers

Avro test pilot Ken Cook taxies out VM305, the prototype T.20, from Woodford Flight Sheds for the aeroplane's maiden flight on 5 August 1947. The machine was evaluated at A&AEE and flew with various trials units before being sold on the civil market as G-APTL in April 1959. It was sold to Iran (see EP-CAA at page 103) in March 1960, but was damaged beyond repair in an accident on 24 September 1950.

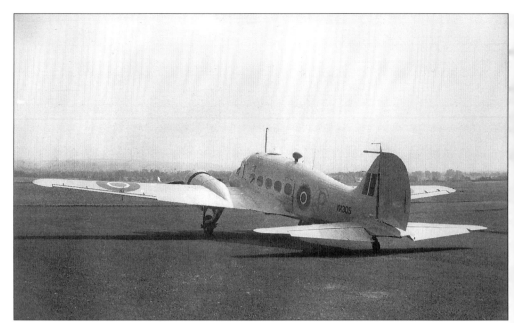

Taken from the C.19 production line, VM305 was converted to the prototype T.20 navigational trainer, designed for use with the RAF's Rhodesia Air Training Group. This type had the hydraulic undercarriage and metal wing and tail unit.

Also taken from the C.19 line was VM306, which was modified to become the prototype of the T.22, a radio trainer version for the RAF. With priority work going into the development of the T.20 for the RAF in Rhodesia, the radio trainer T.22 did not fly for the first time until 21 June 1948, with Ken Cook at the controls once more.

The Anson T.22's cabin was equipped with every type of radio device operated by the RAF at that time. In the foreground is the Direction Finding/Rebecca station with an R.1155 receiver and cabin wall fitted with the DF aerial control. Forward of this station can be seen another R.1155 set, but out of the picture and mounted above the receiver was the well-known T.1154 transmitter. A Gee location station could also be fitted.

Another view of the Anson T.22 prototype at Woodford with an Avro Lincoln parked in the distance. This Anson had the usual evaluation period including a short time with the Fleet Air Arm at Eglington, Northern Ireland, before it was declared surplus in January 1960.

One of a small batch of T.20s in the midst of the C.19 production line was VM413, which went to No.3 Air Navigation School (ANS) at Thornhill, Southern Rhodesia, late in 1948 coded 'ZD'. The aeroplane returned to the UK to serve with No.23 Group Communications Flight and was photographed in 1952 while based at Cranfield, Bedfordshire. It was scrapped in December 1957.

Another of the T.20s of No.3 ANS at Thornhill, 'ZO', VM417, never returned to Britain as it was reduced to spares after an accident. The aircraft landed on an unfinished runway at Kumalo near Bulawayo on 21 August 1950, causing heavy damage after a tyre burst and the tail wheel assembly collapsed.

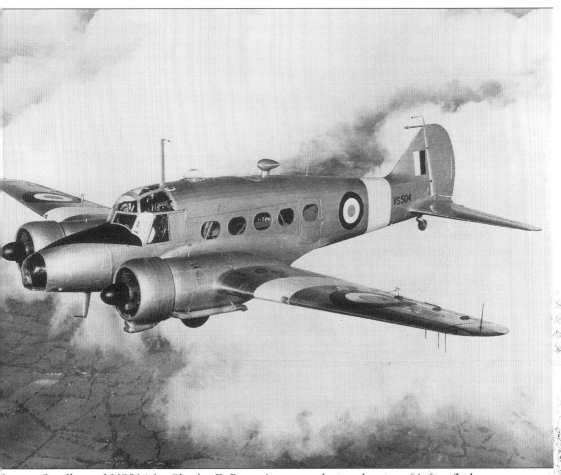

Jimmy Orrell posed VS504 for Charles E. Brown's camera during the aircraft's first flight on 5 February 1948. It was destined not to return to the UK after its service with No.3 ANS in Southern Rhodesia.

In service with No.3 ANS, 'ZZ' VS504 is pushed back into one of Thornhill's hangars in 1949. The aeroplane was en route to a posting in England when it crash landed near Saras in the Sudan on 23 August 1951 and was broken up for scrap.

Having seen RAF service as VS514, this aircraft was sold to Air Couriers at Croydon and registered G-APCF on 5 June 1957. The British registration was cancelled thirteen months later when it was sold in France and given the French overseas registration F-OBIJ, seen here. The aeroplane operated in Algeria until 1966 when it was withdrawn from service.

Photographed at Woodford on 4 June 1948, VS558 awaits collection by the RAF. However, the aircraft was never to serve in the military as it immediately went into storage, not to emerge until nine years later when it was sold as G-APCH. After a year on the British civil register with Air Couriers, the aeroplane followed a number of others to Algeria becoming F-OBHB and ending its days there in 1963.

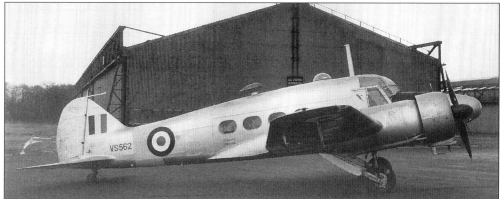

The first Anson T.21 navigation trainer for home use, as opposed to the T.20's operations in Rhodesia, VS562 was photographed at Woodford on 8 April 1962 before it was flown down to Air Service Training for trials with the navigation equipment.

A regular visitor to its ancestral home at Woodford while being operated by the A&AEE at Boscombe Down, VS562 is seen here when it was invited to take part in the Woodford Air Show on 9 July 1966. The fuselage stripe and complete tail unit was painted in day-glow orange. In April 1968 the aircraft was presented to the Air Training Corps at Llanbedr, Wales, with the ground instructional number 8012M.

The Station Flight of Leconfield, Yorkshire operated VS576, the T.21, after it had been released from its navigational duties. It is seen here in one of that station's C-type hangars. The machine was sold for scrap in January 1962.

Since 1920 some interesting aircraft have served as instructional airframes at the RAF's No.1 School of Technical Training at Halton, Buckinghamshire. In May 1953 7016M, formerly VS600, joined the unit. The Anson T.22 had served with a number of radio schools before being grounded and serving the trainees until it was disposed of three months after this photograph was taken on 14 September 1957.

An example of No.2 ANS's strange painting of the unit code-letters 'FFP' with VV245's individual letter being 'B-Baker'. The aircraft's last unit was Allied Air Forces Central Europe before it was scrapped in June 1960.

The pale blue fuselage band of the RAF College at Cranwell is still used today, and is evident on VV247, an Anson T.21 photographed at Blackbushe, Hampshire, on 6 September 1955. The aircraft served with the College for nearly twelve years before being retired in June 1960.

After dropping a passenger, VV250 of No.11 Reserve Flying School (RFS) codes are actually 'RCR-W' based at Scone, Scotland. The aircraft collided with VV250 of the same unit during a formation flight on 15 September 1950 with the former crashing and bursting into flames.

Previous page: Women played a great part in the construction of aircraft during the Second World War, and Avro kept a number to carry on in the manufacturing process. Here, two ladies finish T.21 VV243 in April 1948, lost in a fatal collision with G-AHCW, a BEA Dakota, near Coventry on 19 February 1949. It was operating with No.2 ANS Middleton St George at the time of the accident.

With yet another style of lettering for the unit code, VV261 of No.11 RFS, Scone is actually 'V-Victor'. The aircraft had started life as a T.21, but was converted to a passenger-carrying version designated C.21. It served with a number of navigation and communications units before being sold for scrap in April 1964.

The Reserve Flying Schools discarded the three letter unit code and individual aircraft letter in 1951 in favour of a system of numbers with the No.16 RFS Anson changing from 'RCS-B' to No.11. It operated with the RFS at Burnaston, Derby until June 1953 when it was transferred to RAF Waddington's Station Flight. It was SOC on 17 February 1958.

Not 'R-Roger' but really 'RCR-Z' in another letter style of No.11 RFS at Scone. This T.21, VV299, was the one which survived the collision with VV250 on 15 September 1959, although the Grim Reaper did catch up with the former on 7 May 1953 when it crashed into a hill near Alnwick, Northumberland, in bad visibility.

With the code letters of No.18 RFS based at Fairoaks, Surrey, but carrying the individual number '4' instead of a letter, this aircraft illustrates yet another method of identity marking. VV300's career came to an end when, after a heavy landing at RAF Hendon on 22 May 1958, the undercarriage collapsed.

Avro test pilot Eric Esler takes the Anson T.21 VV313 into the air for the first time at Woodford on 13 October 1948, a day when no fewer than five Ansons took their maiden flight! After service with No.22 RFS at Cambridge the aeroplane was converted to a C.21.

Awaiting the axeman at RAF Shawbury on 20 February 1966 is VV313. Note the movement of the direction finder after its conversion.

No.23 RFS at Usworth, Northumberland, did display its code-letters in the correct style as seen on VV996 'RSA-W' in 1951. The aeroplane operated with that unit until it was disbanded on 31 July 1953. The Anson then went into storage until it was scrapped in 1962.

Leaving the Chadderton factory on a wet day in March 1948, the T.21 VV906 was described as the '8,000th Anson to be built at the Avro factories'. Driver Bob Noon took aircraft sections sixteen miles from Chadderton to Woodford from 1939 until he retired in 1964, and these

included the thirty-six feet wide centre sections of Vulcan jet bombers! This Anson was eventually retired over fourteen years later. The ground floor corner of the building in the right of the photograph now houses Chadderton's excellent Heritage and Visitor Centre.

From 1951, this photograph shows the T.21 WB462, which carries the codes of No.1 RFS at Panshanger, Hertfordshire. When this coding system was dropped later in the same year the aircraft became No.56. It was disposed of in January 1962.

Seen from the Flight Operations office at Woodford, WD402 was visiting Avro on one of the regular liaison flights from A&AEE, Boscombe Down, on 18 May 1964. The aircraft had been converted from a T.21 to a communications C.21 before it was allocated to RAE Llanbedr. In the background are the Club House and one of the 1916 hangars brought to Woodford when the flying field at Alexandra Park, Manchester, closed in 1924.

Landing at Manchester International Airport (Ringway) on 15 May 1983 is the T.21 WD413. The aircraft, restored and kept in flying condition by Mr G.M.K. Fraser, is currently operated by Air Atlantique of Coventry as G-BFIR. It was another conversion from navigation trainer to communications, but at the end of its service it was allocated the instructional number 7881M at No.23 Maintenance Unit at Aldergrove, Northern Ireland in March 1965, before it was sold to Mr Fraser in January 1978.

The Anson T.21 WD416 had served with a number of Navigation Schools after entering service early in 1951, before it joined the Station Flight at Duxford, Cambridgeshire. Here it is taxiing out for take-off at Yeadon (Leeds-Bradford) on 6 June 1960. It was sold for scrap in May 1962.

Accidents will happen! The Lancaster WU-03 for the French Navy rolled down the notorious slope at Woodford's Flight Sheds into the Anson T.21 WJ515 in January 1952. The T.21 had made its first

flight in the capable hands of Avro test pilot Jack Wales on 17 December 1951, before going to the Handling Squadron at A&AEE, Boscombe Down. It was scrapped in May 1960.

Test Pilot Jack Wales captained WJ513 on its maiden flight on 30 November 1951, with the new aircraft joining No.23 RFS at Usworth, Northumberland, two months later. When the unit disbanded in July 1953 the machine was put into storage and, when no new operator was found, the aeroplane was scrapped in June 1960.

In pristine condition, the T.21 WJ553 nears the end of its days, sadly going for fire practice at St Mawgan, Cornwall, in December 1962.

Avro chief test pilot Jimmy Orrell said, 'I pulled rank to fly the last Anson' and he did so on 13 May 1952. He thought of it as one of the highlights of his long career, during which he test flew 1,314 aircraft including 917 Lancasters and118 Ansons. Of the total, ten were prototypes.

A peaceful scene at Woodford in May 1952 with the 10,996th and last Anson awaiting its first test flight. Next to it is the Avro 707B VX790 and a Lincoln bomber is parked in the distance.

*Following pages:*Jimmy Orrell flies the T.21 WJ561 past Woodford during its maiden flight on 13 May 1952. On the airfield are five white-painted Lancasters and a York transport aircraft.

Signing off! Jimmy Orrell banks away from the camera aircraft before landing back at Woodford. In a special ceremony at Woodford on 27 May 1952, Avro supremo Sir Roy Dobson handed over WJ561 to Wing Commander H. Budden, who was on hand to do what thousands had done before him – accept an Anson on behalf of the RAF!